EARTH IN DANGER!

Transport

Polly Goodman

HODDER
Wayland

Titles in the **EARTH IN DANGER!** series

Coasts   Rivers

Energy   Settlements

Farming   Transport

For more information on this series and other Hodder Wayland titles, go to www.hodderwayland.co.uk

This book is a simplified version of the title *Transport* in Hodder Wayland's 'Earth Alert' series.

Language level consultant: Norah Granger
Editor: Belinda Hollyer
Designer: Jane Hawkins

First published in 2001 by Hodder Wayland,
an imprint of Hodder Children's Books.

This paperback edition published in 2005

Britian Library Cataloguing in Publication Data
Goodman, Polly
Transport. - (Earth in danger!)
1.Transportation - Environmental aspects - Juvenile literature
I.Title
333.7'968
ISBN 0 7502 4725 8

Printed in China by WKT Company Limited

Hodder Children's Books
A division of Hodder Headline Limited
338 Euston Road, London NW1 3BH

Picture acknowledgements
Cover: main picture Tony Stone/Bruce Hands, plane Tony Stone/George Hunter; Axiom Photographic Agency (Steve Benbow) 23, (Steve Benbow) 25, (Jim Holmes) 26; James Davis Travel Photography 20; Ecoscene (Melanie Peters) 8, 13, (John Farmar) 28; Eye Ubiquitous (Julia Bayne) 7; (J.C. Pasieka) 21; Foster and Partners 29 both; Hodder Wayland Picture Library (Julia Waterlow) 3, 5, 16, 18, Impact Photos (Charles Coates) 4, (Christophe Bluntzer) 6, (Trevor Morgan) 12, (Alain Evrard) 24; Tony Stone Images (Paul Chesley) cover, (Baron Wolman) 1, (Don Smetzer) 10, (Richard Brown) 11, (David Woodfall) 14, (Will & Deni McIntyre) 15, (George Hunter) 22; (A. Blackburn) 19.

Artwork by Peter Bull Art Studio.

Contents

What is transport?

Everybody needs transport – to get to school or work, to go shopping, or to go on holiday. Transport is the action of moving people or goods from one place to another.

There are many different types of transport, from jumbo jets to skateboards, and from paddle boats to supertankers. They travel over land, water or through the air.

Transport and energy

All transport uses energy. Some uses energy produced by coal or oil, such as cars, motorbikes and aeroplanes. Other types of transport use energy from the sun or the wind, or from the muscles of people and animals.

Bicycles, cars, buses and animals are all types of transport in this Indian street. ▼

Environmental damage

Any type of transport that is used too much can damage the environment. Too many cars produce pollution and traffic jams, and use up the world's oil supplies. Too many walkers or mountain bikers can wear away footpaths.

Today, people are using transport more often and for longer distances than ever before. We have to be careful about the types of transport we use and know how much damage they cause.

HISTORY OF TRANSPORT

c.5000 BC	Donkeys and oxen first used
c.3500 BC	Mesopotamians built the first wheels
c.3200 BC	Egyptians invented sails
1769–1813	First steam engines (trains and boats)
1880s	First petrol engines
1903	First aeroplane
1920s	Cars became popular
1950s	First commercial jet aeroplanes
1961	First person travelled in space

▲ Skateboards are a type of wheeled transport. The first wheels were built about 5,500 years ago.

Transport without engines

Before engines were invented about 200 years ago, the main forms of transport were walking, sailing or using animals. Walking and animal transport use power made by muscles. Sailing uses power produced by the wind.

Oxen, horses, bullocks and yaks are still used to pull vehicles and carry loads in many parts of the world today, especially on farms in poorer countries. Sailing boats are also still used, but mostly for sport or fun.

Horse-drawn carts in Romania.▼

Bicycles

Bicycles also use energy from muscles. The muscles in our legs push the pedals, which push the wheels.

Bicycles are used for sports, such as mountain biking and road cycling. But they are also a good way to travel short distances.

Cycling is a cheap and healthy way to get around. It is also a harmless type of transport because it doesn't burn oil to make energy.

▲ BMX and mountain bikes on a cycle route.

Food journeys

Forty years ago, most people bought food from their local shop or market. Many food shops were in town centres, where people could walk to them.

Today, many supermarkets have moved to the edges of towns and cities, so people have to make car journeys to buy their food.

Food can also be sent long distances to reach supermarkets.

Lots of foods, like bananas, pineapples and dates, are grown in hot countries and shipped thousands of miles to supermarkets.

All these journeys cause damage to the environment because they use a lot of energy and cause pollution.

◀ Unpacking a car after a supermarket shopping trip.

BICYCLE HIRE

In Amsterdam, the capital city of the Netherlands, there is a new type of public transport using bicycles.

Special bicycles are controlled by a computer system. People use a card, like a credit card, to hire a bicycle. The computer gives them a print-out of their route. At their destination, places are reserved for them to leave their bikes.

The DEPO system, as it is called, reduces the number of car and bus journeys in Amsterdam. It means there are fewer traffic jams, the air is cleaner and the city is less noisy.

People hiring a bike at a DEPO station in Amsterdam.▼

Choosing transport

In wealthy countries, most of us can choose how to make short journeys. We can walk, cycle, drive a car or take a bus.

Sometimes cars and buses can be faster, and they can help us carry shopping and heavy bags. But if the roads are very busy, cycling or even walking can be quicker.

Many people drive cars over short distances when they could cycle or walk instead. In Britain, most car journeys are under 8 kilometres.

Safe routes

To increase cycling and walking, countries need safe routes. Walkers, disabled people and parents with prams need smooth pavements and ramps. Cyclists need cycle lanes to separate them from traffic.

◀ Well-kept pavements are safe routes for everyone.

Activity

Find out how your class travel to school, using a map. Ask your teacher to help.

1. Find a map of your local area.
2. Cover the map with tracing paper and mark the position of your school.

3. Ask each class member to mark their homes on the map using the following symbols:

● If they walk to school, draw a pair of shoes.

● If they travel by car, draw a car.

● If they take a bus, draw a bus.

▲ A school bus in the USA.

4. Draw lines from each home to your school and measure the distances of each.
5. Use the table on page 8 to find out how much energy each person uses to get to school.

Cars, buses and trains

Cars, buses and trains are quicker than walking or cycling. They can also carry heavier loads. Most use energy produced by burning petrol or diesel oil. Oil is a fossil fuel which is taken from under the ground.

FOSSIL FUELS

Oil, coal and gas are called fossil fuels. They were formed underground millions of years ago from the remains of plants and animals. Fossil fuels are being used up rapidly.

Burning oil causes air pollution and uses up the earth's energy supplies. Some experts say that if we keep on using the same amounts of oil, there will be very little left in fifty years' time.

Trains and trams

Some trains burn diesel oil to produce energy. Other trains and trams run on electricity. Electricity can be produced by burning coal, or by using wind or water power.

Trams use electricity for energy, which creates less air pollution in streets. ▶

Cars

Cars are the most common form of transport in the world. More and more people own cars every day.

Cars are very convenient. They take people where they want to go, when they want to go there.

Many people choose to drive, even if they could choose public transport instead.▼

For people who live in areas where there is no public transport, and for some disabled people, cars are essential. Car-owners can make short journeys, or long journeys, one after the other. Many people feel safer in cars than on buses and trains.

NUMBER OF CARS
There are about 750 million cars in the world today.

POLLUTION FROM CARS

Gases from exhaust pipes cause pollution. Some gases form a smog in the air. Others mix with water in the clouds and fall in rain. This is called acid rain.

Fumes from a car exhaust pipe.▼

Damage from cars

When cars burn petrol or diesel, they cause air pollution, which can make it difficult for some people to breathe properly.

Cars also release gases that rise up into the earth's atmosphere. These 'greenhouse' gases keep the earth warm. As we burn more fossil fuels, many scientists are worried that the earth will get hotter. If this happens, it could cause serious problems. Droughts could cause famine, sea levels could rise and cause floods, and many species of plants and animals would die.

14

Traffic jams

As more and more people use cars, roads are getting busier. Many become blocked by traffic jams. In the morning and evening rush hours, traffic can stand still for hours.

When cars stand still with their engines running, air pollution increases. So traffic jams increase air pollution.

▲This roundabout has been blocked by a traffic jam.

Activity

TRAFFIC SURVEY

1. Ask an adult to help, and choose a busy road near your school.

2. Spend 15 minutes making a record of every car that goes past and the number of passengers inside.

3. Draw a bar graph showing your information, with a different bar for each number of passengers.

4. Which bar is longest? How could you reduce the amount of cars on the street?

Public transport

Public transport such as buses, trains and trams can reduce the number of cars on roads. Each vehicle carries a large number of people, so less energy is used up per person (see the table on page 8). So public transport can reduce damage to the environment.

People will only choose to use public transport if it is cheap, near their homes, and easy to use.

▲ A train in Argentina.

Some people think that governments should spend more money on improving public transport than on building roads.

Beth and Mark Malallieu live with their four children in Luray, a small town in Virginia, USA.

Mark drives 45 kilometres to work every day and Beth drives 1.6 kilometres. Their three elder children walk to school, 5 minutes away.

Beth says: 'I could cycle to work, but I have to drop Thomas off at his child-minder first. I just wouldn't feel safe coming home on a bike late at night.'

Mark says there is no public transport in their area: 'There are no local buses and the nearest coach station is 32 kilometres away. Everyone we know around here has a car, and most people have two.'

The Malallieu family have two cars, which are used every day. ▼

Long-distance transport

Cars can be used to travel long distances, but trains or aeroplanes can be quicker. They can also be very expensive.

Transporting goods

Goods are transported around countries using lorries, trains, aeroplanes and boats. Each type of transport has a different speed, cost and ability to carry big loads.

Boats are the cheapest way to carry heavy goods, but they are also the slowest. Lorries and trains are faster but more expensive. Lorries take goods straight to their destination.

Aeroplanes are the fastest transport, but they are very expensive and not good for heavy loads.

These heavy goods are being transported on the Rhine river, in Germany. ▼

Damage from lorries, trains and boats

Boats cause the least damage to the environment. Since they carry large loads, they use less energy for each tonne of goods.

Lorries cause the most harm. They create air pollution and cause traffic jams. Since each lorry carries fewer goods than a big boat, they use up more energy for each tonne of goods.

▲ Aeroplane fuel pollutes the air.

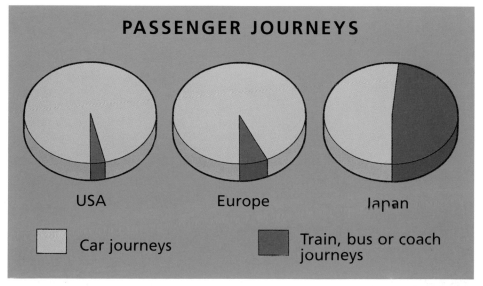

PASSENGER JOURNEYS

USA   Europe   Japan

☐ Car journeys   ☐ Train, bus or coach journeys

Activity

MEASURING CAPACITY

Every road has a maximum number of vehicles it can carry quickly and safely. This is its capacity. If roads carry more vehicles than their capacity, they become congested and accidents can happen.

1. Place two chairs 2 metres apart. This is your 'road'.
2. Ask four people in your class to walk quickly between the chairs as many times as possible for 1 minute without touching each other. Did they succeed?
3. Now increase the number of people until they start bumping into each other. When they do, you have reached the capacity of the 'road'.
4. Repeat the experiment moving the chairs 3 metres apart. Does the capacity get bigger?

Roads can be widened to increase their capacity. This would affect the local environment.

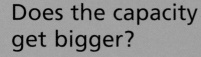

◀ A congested street in Delhi, India.

Developing countries

Poorer countries have fewer roads and railways. The only way to travel long distances is often by river, or on small aeroplanes. Only wealthy people can afford to fly.

TRUE STORY

TRANSPORT IN A RAIN FOREST

Eugenie and Jean Ivombo live with their children in a small town in Gabon, West Africa. Eugenie's parents live 380 kilometres away, in the middle of the rain forest.

To visit Eugenie's parents, the family can take a bush taxi, or fly to a small airstrip in the rain forest. Driving takes 10 hours since the roads are very bumpy.

If there were better roads in the rain forest, it would make life easier for many people in Gabon. But farmers would probably use the roads to move in and cut down the trees. Then the rain forest could be destroyed.

The Ivombo family.▼

New roads built in the rain forest would destroy rare species of plants and animals. ▶

International transport

Most goods travelling between countries are carried by ships. Many goods are put in large metal containers and carried on container ships. Supertankers up to 450 metres long carry oil.

Tourism

Since the 1960s, air travel has got much cheaper and many more people are now going abroad for their holidays. Tourism can help areas by bringing in money and creating jobs. Facilities such as shops and roads can be improved for local people. Tourism can help people understand different cultures.

◄ Many people from rich countries visit other countries on holiday.

Damage from tourism

Too many tourists can also cause a lot of damage. Waste from large hotels can pollute beaches and seas, destroying coral reefs and killing fish. Sports such as waterskiing and diving can also disturb wildlife.

Ancient buildings can be damaged by too many visitors. Eventually, tourism can ruin beautiful places so that tourists do not want to visit them any more.

Local people can suffer from tourism, too. Tourists can change traditional ways of life and introduce foreign diseases.

▲ A polluted beach in Spain.

MEDITERRANEAN TOURISM

Every year, over 160 million tourists visit the Mediterranean region. New buildings have destroyed hundreds of kilometres of sand dunes between Gibraltar and Sicily. Hotel-building in southern Turkey was destroying the habitat of the loggerhead turtle. Building work was stopped and the area is now protected.

BALI

Bali is an island in Indonesia, with a warm climate. Over 3.5 million people live on Bali. Most people are Hindus, who hold religious festivals throughout each year.

▲ A new hotel in Bali.

In 1966, the first big beach hotel was built on the island, with running water, electricity and elevators. Since then, large numbers of tourists have been visiting Bali. Over 350,000 people now fly to the island every year.

Builders are constantly at work on new sites for hotels, shops, restaurants and nightclubs, and there are many new roads.

Local people have made lots of money from tourism. But the island has been changed for ever.

Careful tourism

It is possible to visit other countries without damaging them. Careful tourists try not to damage the wildlife and landscape. They respect local people's cultures and try not to change them.

▲ A lizard takes a look at some tourists in South America. The tourists are learning about the local wildlife.

Activity

HOW TO BE A GOOD TOURIST

Imagine some children are coming to visit you. They live deep in a rain forest, on the other side of the world, where their way of life is very different.

Prepare an information pack for them about the things they will need to know. Include information about transport, and about safety on the roads. What will they need to wear? What are the best places for them to visit? What other advice will be useful?

The future

To protect our environment, we need to reduce the amount of energy used in transport, or find new sources of energy to replace fossil fuels.

We need to try to reduce the number of car journeys, so there is less air pollution and fewer traffic jams. Car journeys can be reduced if more people use public transport, share car journeys with others, and walk or cycle short distances. Governments can help by spending money on public transport, pavements and cycle routes, to encourage people not to drive.

Computers and the Internet
Computers are reducing the amount of travelling people do all over the world and helping to reduce pollution.

There is no pavement for these children in Japan, so it is not safe for them to walk to school. ▶

Email and the Internet allow people to work from home instead of travelling to an office, and documents can be sent electronically using email instead of using postal transport.

Business meetings between companies on different sides of the world can now take place using video links, which reduce the amount of air travel.

Internet shopping allows people to buy goods using their computer and have them delivered to their home, without stepping out of their front door.

▲ Buying food at local shops is better for the environment, because it uses less energy than travelling to a shopping centre.

New sources of fuel

Experts are trying to find new sources of energy to replace oil. Fuel called ethanol is being produced from sugar-cane pulp in Brazil. Cars are being made with solar panels, which create energy from the sun's rays. Electric motors would cause less air pollution, especially if the electricity was produced by power stations using solar or wind power.

New inventions need to be cheap enough for everyone to afford, including people in poorer countries, because pollution in one country affects the whole planet.

This car in Australia is covered with solar panels.▼

Parliament Square as it is today, showing Big Ben and the Houses of Parliament. ▼

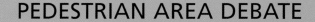

PEDESTRIAN AREA DEBATE

Officials in London are planning to make parts of Parliament Square pedestrian areas.

Find out about the different points of view that might be involved by taking part in this debate.

Among a group of friends, choose one of the roles below. In turn, spend 5 minutes talking about how the decision to pedestrianize Parliament Square will affect you.

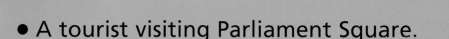

- A tourist visiting Parliament Square.
- A local café owner.
- A disabled person who uses a wheelchair, who wants to visit Parliament Square.
- A van driver delivering to customers in the area.

◀ This photo has been altered to show Parliament Square as a pedestrianized area.

Glossary

Acid rain Rain that contains pollution.

Droughts Long periods of dry weather, or lack of rain.

Exhaust pipe A pipe underneath cars. Gases, or exhaust fumes, travel from the engine out through the exhaust pipe.

Fossil fuels Natural fuels including coal, oil and natural gas which formed underground millions of years ago from the remains of plants and animals.

Megajoules Energy is measured in joules. Megajoules are thousands of joules.

Pedestrian areas Pedestrian areas are closed to cars. Only pedestrians, bicycles and emergency vehicles are allowed in them.

Pedestrianize To make a road or an area only for pedestrians.

Rush hours The times in the mornings and evenings when people travel to and from work.

Smog A mixture of smoke and fog.

Solar panels Panels that absorb the sun's rays and help convert them into energy for heating or electricity.

Solar power Power produced from the sun's rays.

Supertankers Very large ships.

Wind power Energy from the wind, which can be used by sailing boats and to make electricity.

Further information

MUSIC
- Rhythms/sounds of transport forms
- Songs about journeys and travelling

GEOGRAPHY
- Comparing and grouping different forms of transport
- Scale of journeys
- Map work
- Environmental, economic and social effects
- Links between places

HISTORY
- Changing forms of transport
- Role of transport in social/economic development

ART & CRAFT
- Drawing street scenes and transport
- Postcards and travel posters

Topic Web

DESIGN & TECHNOLOGY
- Designing and constructing boats, vehicles and flying machines

MATHS
- Recording, manipulating and analysing data
- Graphs and diagrams

SCIENCE
- Sources and uses of transport energy
- Human body and movement
- Motion, capacity and congestion
- Managing experiments

ENGLISH
- Stories and poems about journeys
- Writing about travel and tourism

Other books to read

Environment Starts Here!: Transport by Andrew & Amanda Church (Hodder Wayland, 2001)

A Century of Change: Transport by Jane Shuter (Heinemann, 2000)

Future Tech: Transport by Nick Arnold (Belitha, 1999)

Children's Encyclopedia of Transport: On the Move by Ian Graham (Marshall Editions, 2001)

Picture Reference: Transport by David Glover (TwoCan, 2000)

Saving our World: New Energy Sources by N. Hawkes (Franklin Watts, 2003)

Speedy Machines series: Bikes, Boats, Cars by Vic Parker (Belitha, 2000)

Great Inventions: Transport by Paul Dowswell (Heinemann, 2002)

Sustainable World: Transport by Rob Bowden (Hodder Wayland, 2003)

World's Worst: Shipping Disasters by Rob Alcraft (Heinemann, 2000)

Index